Clara Barton

Teacher, Nurse, Leader

Dona Herweck Rice

Clara Barton helped others.

Clara's house

She helped her sick brother.

She helped young children learn.

Think and Talk

How does your teacher help you?

Clara

She helped women earn better pay.

She helped men in the army who were hurt.

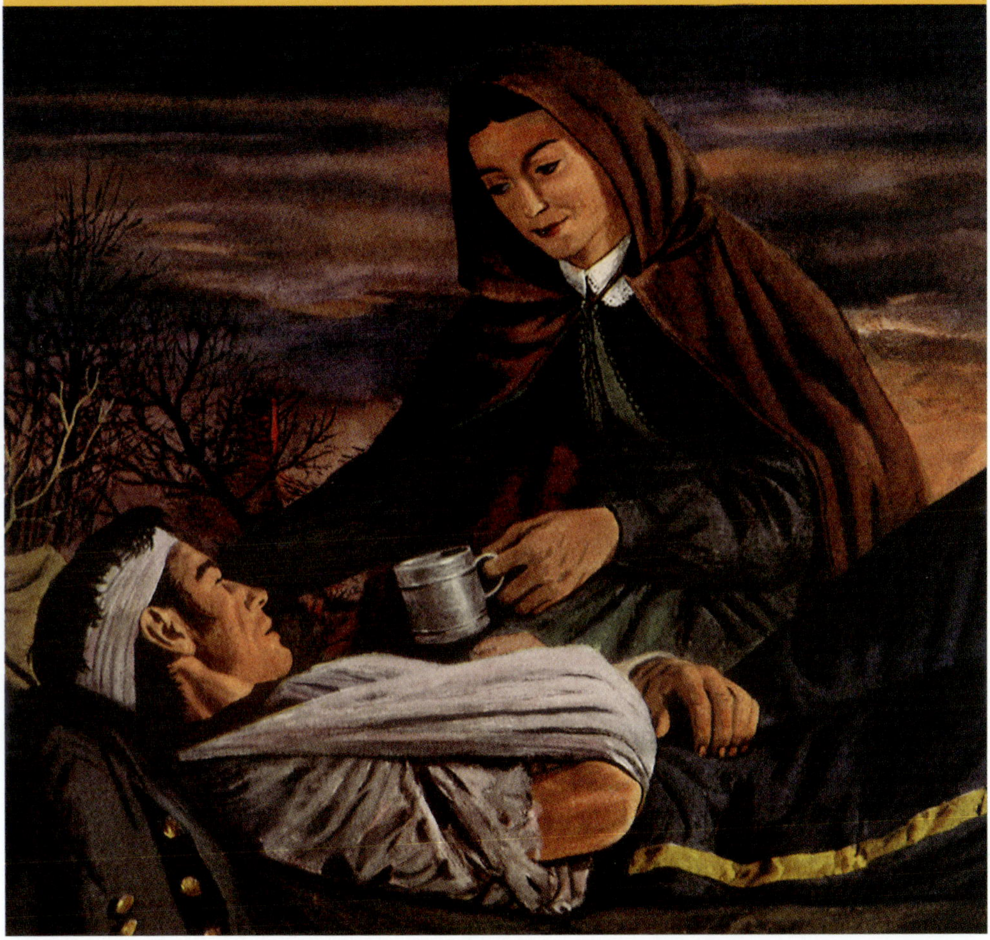

She helped the Red Cross overseas.

She started the Red Cross at home.

Clara made the world a better place.

Jump into Fiction

Clara Helps

The piglet was in trouble.

"Do not worry," Clara said. "I will help you."

Civics in Action

Each of us can do things to help others. We can pick up trash. We can make a card for a sick person. There is a lot we can do.

1. Think about one thing you can do to help others.

2. Plan for how you will help.

3. Share your plan.